FRANCISCO
AND JACINTA

Little Shepherds of Our Lady

Secretariado dos Pastorinhos
FÁTIMA

Imprimatur,
Fatima, 13th May 2008
† Antonio, Bishop of Leiria-Fatima

Compiled by
        Fr. Luis Kondor SVD
in collaboration with
        Ana Câmara and Manuel V. Cruz
Illustrations by
        Mercês and Júlio Gil
Translated by
        Dominican Nuns
        of Mosteiro de Santa Maria (Lisbon)

Cover Picture: Our Lady takes
the two Little Shepherds with Her to Heaven.

*Suffer the little children to come unto me
and forbid them not.* (Mt 19,14)

*Truly I say to you, unless you turn
and become like children,
you will never enter the kingdom of heaven.* (Mt 18,3)

*I thank thee, Father, Lord of heaven and earth,
for revealing to little ones
the mysteries of the Kingdom.* (Mt 11,25)

(From the Mass for Blessed
Francisco and Jacinta Marto)

Dear Children,

The paths of life you will have to tread in this
third millennium may well be much more
difficult than in the past. For this reason, God
is putting before you the example of two holy
children: Francisco and Jacinta of Fatima.
They can give you courage when you think
about them. As heroes, they will always be
an example with their faith, hope and love.

Francisco and Jacinta were brother and sister
and they were born in Aljustrel,
a little village on a range of hills near Fatima
called Serra d'Aire.
Their parents lost no time in taking
each of them to the Church
to be made children of God.
Francisco was born on 11th June 1908
and was baptised ten days later, on 20th June.
Jacinta was born on 11th March, 1910,
and was baptised eight days later.

As the two children grew up they became
very fond of their cousin, Lucia,
who lived nearby.

Jacinta was a merry little girl, who loved
to dance and play.
But she always wanted to be the one
to choose the games, and she used to sulk
when she did not get her way.

Francisco was different: very quiet,
and rather easy-going; he loved to sing
and play the flute,
and to live at peace with everyone.
When playing games,
it never bothered him if he lost.

One day someone gave him a handkerchief
with the image of Our Lady of Nazaré
painted on it. He was delighted
and showed it to the other children.
They passed it from on to another
until it suddenly disappeared...
but Lucia saw it hidden away
in another boy's pocket,
who was refusing to give it back.
When Lucia tried to snatch it from him,
Francisco intervened and said: 'Forget it!
What does a handkerchief matter to me?'

Like St Francis of Assisi,
Francisco was very fond of animals.
One day, another boy caught a sparrow. Dis-
tressed, Francisco promised to give him
two small coins if he would let it go.
The other boy accepted the offer,
but wanted the money at once.
Francisco ran all the way home
to get the money.
When he saw the bird flying off,
he clapped his hands
and called out to it: 'Be careful!
Don't let yourself get caught again!'

When Lucia began minding
her parents' sheep,
Francisco and Jacinta asked their mother
if they, too, could be shepherds
and mind their own flock
together with their cousin's.
In order to imitate Our Lord
in a picture that she had of Him,
Jacinta loved to carry the lambs in her arms
so that they didn't get tired.

When the three children were together,
however much time they had,
it seemed too little for all the games
they wanted to play.
After they had eaten their sandwich lunch,
they did as their mothers had told them:
they joined their hands and prayed the rosary.
But they speeded things up
by saying just 'Hail Mary', 'Hail Mary' ...
with only the words 'Our Father'
at the end of every decade.
It was a very quick rosary indeed!

But ever since they were very small,
at home and in church,
they had learned to love God.
Once, when they were playing
a game of forfeits,
Jacinta took the crucifix down from the wall
in order to give Our Lord
three kisses and three hugs.

One day, Lucia and Jacinta were in a
procession, dressed as angels, in white,
close to the canopy, strewing flowers in front
of Jesus [in the Blessed Sacrament],
being carried by the Parish Priest.
But in spite of the signs Lucia kept making
to her, Jacinta was not strewing her flowers,
just looking at the priest.
Afterwards she explained why:
'I didn't see Him', she said.
Lucia explained to her that Jesus was hidden
in the Host. From then on, they always
referred to Our Lord in the Blessed
Sacrament as the 'hidden Jesus'.

One day in Spring, in the shelter of a rock
known as Loca do Cabeço,
they ate their lunch
and then said the Rosary as usual.
They had already begun to play,
when they saw a young man
coming towards them, as white as snow,
and telling them not to be afraid,
because he was the Angel of Peace.
He then knelt down,
bent right down to the ground
and told them to say the following prayer:
– **My God, I believe, I adore, I hope, I love
you. I ask pardon of you for those who do
not believe, do not hope and do not love you.**
They repeated this prayer three times.
As he did not hear the voice of the Angel,
Francisco repeated the prayer
after the two girls.
Before he disappeared, the Angel said to them:
– **Pray thus. The Hearts of Jesus and Mary
are attentive to the voice of your
supplications.**

In the summer, beside the well
in Lucia's garden, the Angel appeared again
and said to them:
– **What are you doing! Pray, pray very
much!**
**The hearts of Jesus and Mary have
designs of mercy on you. Offer prayers
and sacrifices constantly to the Most High.**
At Lucia's request, the Angel explained to
them that they were to make of everything
they could a sacrifice, in reparation for the
sins which offend God so much
and in petition for the conversion of sinners.
He also said:
– **You will thus draw down peace upon
your country. I am its Angel Guardian,
the Angel of Portugal. Above all, accept
and bear with submission the suffering
which the Lord will send you.**

The Angel appeared to them a third time.
This time, he held a chalice in his hand,
and above it a Host, from which drops
of blood were falling into the Chalice.
Leaving the Chalice and the Host suspended
in the air, he knelt down and bowed low,
and then repeated the following prayer
three times:

**– Most Holy Trinity, Father, Son
and Holy Spirit, I adore you profoundly,
and I offer You the most precious Body,
Blood, Soul and Divinity of Jesus Christ,
present in all the tabernacles of the world,
in reparation for the outrages,
sacrileges and indifferences
with which He Himself
is offended. And, through the infinite me-
rits of his Most Sacred Heart,
and the Immaculate Heart of Mary,
I beg of You the conversion
of poor sinners.**

He then stood up and gave the Host to Lucia
and offered the Chalice to Jacinta
and Francisco to drink from, saying:
–**Take and drink the Body and Blood
of Jesus Christ, horribly outraged
by ungrateful men. Make reparation
for their crimes and console your God.**
Lying flat on the ground, the children
repeated three times the prayer
the Angel of Peace had taught them.

On 13 May 1917, the three little shepherds
took the sheep to the Cova da Iria.
Seeing a flash of lightning, they decided
to return home.
Then there was a second flash of lightning,
and they suddenly saw a Lady, brighter
than the Sun, dressed all in white,
just above a small holm oak that grew there.
The Lady told them not to be afraid
as She would do them no harm
and that She had come from Heaven.
She added:
– I have come to ask you to come here
for six months in succession, on the 13th
of each month at this time.
Later on I will tell you who I am
and what I want. Afterwards I will return
here yet a seventh time.

Lucia asked:

And shall I go to heaven too?
And Jacinta?... And Francisco?
– Yes – replied the Lady, and then went on
to ask the children the following question:
– **Are you willing to offer yourselves to
God and bear all the sufferings
He wills to send you,
as an act of reparation for the sins
by which He is offended,
and of supplication for the conversion
of sinners?**
– Yes, we are willing – Lucia replied,
speaking for all three of them.
– **Then you are going to have much to
suffer, but the grace of God will be your
comfort... Pray the Rosary every day in
order to obtain peace for the world,
and the end of the war.**

Lucia warned her cousins not to tell anyone
what had happened; but Jacinta was so
thrilled at the sight of the 'beautiful Lady'
that she could not keep the secret
and that night told everything
that had happened to her family at home.
The next day she apologised:
– There was something inside me
that wouldn't let me keep quiet,
she said, with tears in her eyes.

The news spread.
Lucia's mother was upset as she thought
they were going around deceiving people,
and she did everything she could
to make her daughter confess
that she had lied; she even used the handle
of the sweeping brush on her...
But the children could not deny
what they had seen and heard.
This is what they said to the Parish Priest
when he questioned them.
These were the first sufferings
that Our Lady had told them about.

On 13 June, Our Lady asked the children to come again on 13th of the following month, to pray the Rosary every day, and to learn to read. She also promised that she would soon take Jacinta and Francisco with Her to Heaven, but told Lucia that she would have to remain some time longer, because Jesus wished to make use of her to make Our Lady known and loved.

– He wants to establish in the world devotion to my Immaculate Heart. I promise salvation to those who embrace it, and those souls will be loved by God like flowers placed by me to adorn His throne.

And to console Lucia, She also said to her:

– Don't lose heart. I will never forsake you. My Immaculate Heart will be your refuge and the way that will lead you to God.

She then opened her hands and from them streamed rays of intense light. Jacinta and Francisco seemed to be in that part of the light which rose towards heaven, while Lucia was in the part which was poured out on the earth. They also saw the Immaculate Heart of Mary surrounded by thorns and seeking reparation.

The three children began to do
what Our Lady had asked:
to pray and to make sacrifices
for the conversion of sinners.
They used to give their lunch away
to poor children, went for long periods
without drinking water on very hot days;
ate acorns and green olives which were very
bitter; they refused offers of luscious grapes
and figs, and they even let their legs get stung
by nettles and used to wear a thick,
coarse rope tied round their waist...

On 13 July, the Lady came again to ask them
to continue going there on the 13th of each
month, and to pray the Rosary every day
for peace in the world. She promised that
she would tell them in October
who She was and what She wanted,
and a miracle would take place
so that everybody would believe.
She said:
– **Sacrifice yourselves for sinners,
and say many times, especially
whenever you make some sacrifice:
O Jesus, it is for love of You,
for the conversion of sinners,
and in reparation for the sins committed
against the Immaculate Heart of Mary.**

She then showed them Hell, where the souls
of poor sinners go, and she taught them that,
in order to save these souls, God wanted
to establish in the world devotion
to the Immaculate Heart of Mary.
If Her requests were carried out, many souls
would be saved and there would be peace.
But if people did not stop offending God,
many punishments would come upon
the world, with wars, and persecutions
of the Church and of the Holy Father, etc...
However, She promised that in the end Her
Immaculate Heart would triumph.
This was part of the secret which at that time
Our Lady warned them not to reveal to
anyone. She also taught them to add, at the
end of each mystery of the Rosary, the
following prayer:
– O my Jesus, forgive us,
save us from the fire of hell.
Lead all souls to Heaven,
especially those who are most in need.

Finally, on Our Lady's left, the three children
saw an angel with a flaming sword which was
sending out flames in every direction,
as if to set the world on fire;
but the flames were quenched
by the splendour that radiated towards
the angel from Our Blessed Lady's hands.
They also saw, as if in a mirror, a Bishop
dressed in white, who seemed to them to be
the Holy Father. Together with other bishops,
priests and religious, this Bishop was climbing
a steep mountain, at the top of which was
a huge cross. Before he reached the top,
the Pope passed through a great city half in
ruins, and he blessed the bodies of the many
people who had fallen dead by the roadside.
When he reached the top of the mountain, he
was himself killed by a group of soldiers who
fired bullets and arrows at him.
Jacinta was so impressed by this vision that from
the onwards, whenever she offered a sacrifice, she
would say that it was also for the Holy Father.

In 1917 there was serious religious
persecution in Portugal.
The Administrator of the Council of Vila
Nova de Ourem wanted to put an end to all
the tales he was hearing about the apparitions
so he sent for the little shepherds
in order to interrogate them.
As Franciso and Jacinta were so little,
only Lucia went.
But so deep was the friendship
between the three children
that her cousins were very worried about her.
When Lucia returned, at nightfall,
she found them on their knees beside the
well, crying and praying for her.

On 13 August, the children could not go
to the Cova da Iria
as the Administrator came
and took them with him
to Vila Nova de Ourem.
There, first in the Administration building,
then in his own house,
and finally in the prison,
he first made them promises
and then uttered threats
in an effort to get the secret out of them.

In the prison, to comfort them, the other
prisoners urged them to tell the secret,
saying that the fact that the Lady did
not want them to did not really matter;
but the children were brave
and did not let themselves be convinced.
They decided to say the Rosary.
Jacinta took a medal
which she had round her neck,
and asked one of the prisoners
to hang it on a nail in the wall.
They knelt down in front of the medal,
and the other prisoners knelt down too,
and said the Rosary with them.

Then came the worst threat of all.
Pretending that he was heating up
a cauldron of oil in which to fry them
if they did not reveal the secret,
the Administrator sent a guard to fetch
the children, one by one,
in order to frighten them even more.
First Jacinta went, then Francisco,
and finally Lucia.
The children faced the trial with courage.
They neither revealed the secret
nor did they deny what they had seen,
offering it all up as a sacrifice.
At last they were set free, on 15 August,
the Feast of the Assumption of Our Lady.

On 19 August, Our Lady appeared to them
in a place called the Valinhos.
She told them to continue coming
to the Cova da Iria on 13th of each month,
and to pray the Rosary,
and She renewed Her promise of a miracle
on the last day. She then told them
what they were to do with the offerings
 people were leaving at the Cova da Iria.
– Have two litters made. One is to be carried
by you and Jacinta and two other girls dressed
in white; the other one is to be carried
by Francisco and three other boys.
The money from the litters is for the feast
of Our Lady of the Rosary, and what is over
will help towards the construction of a chapel
that you are to have built
Then She added:
– **Pray, pray very much,**
and make sacrifices for sinners;
for many souls go to hell
because there is no-one to make sacrifices
and to pray for them.

On 13 September, the little shepherds
were surrounded by a great many people.
This time Our Lady said:
– **Continue to pray the Rosary**
in order to obtain the end of the war.
In October Our Lord will come too,
as well as Our Lady of Sorrows
and Our Lady of Carmel.
Saint Joseph will appear with the Child
Jesus to bless the world.
God is pleased with your sacrifices.
He does not want you to sleep
with the rope on,
but only wear it during the daytime.
Lucia presented many petitions
and Our Lady replied:
– **Yes, I will cure some but not others.**
In October I will perform a miracle
so that all may believe.

On 13 October there was torrential rain.
When She appeared, Our Lady said:
**– I want to tell you that a chapel
is to be built here in my honour.
I am the Lady of the Rosary.
Continue always to pray the Rosary
every day. The war is going to end,
and the soldiers will soon return
to their homes.**
When Lucia again presented
various requests for cures,
Our Lady replied:
**– Some yes, but not others.
They must amend their lives
and ask forgiveness for their sins.
Do not offend the Lord God any more,
because He is already so much offended.**

The promised miracle then took place.
Opening Her hands,
the Lady made the light from them
reflect on the sun.
The rain stopped suddenly,
the crowd looked up at the sky
and was terrified to see the sun tremble,
turn about on itself and, in a violent dance,
appear to be going to fall to earth
out of the sky, with multi-coloured rays
of light shooting from it in every direction.
– Miracle – the people cried, and many
begged pardon for their sins.
This was how God put His divine seal
on the apparitions in Fatima.
While all this was happening, the little
shepherds saw visions of the Holy Family,
Our Lady of Sorrows
and Our Lady of Mount Carmel.

Francisco was very moved
when the Angel asked them to console God.
From then on he used to try to slip away
quietly on his own
so that he could be recollected
and think about Our Lord.
Sometimes, Lucia and Jacinta found him
kneeling down, absorbed in prayer,
and unaware of what was happening
around him.

He spent as much time as he could in church,
in adoration before the Blessed Sacrament,
and when he became ill
his great sorrow was that he could no longer
visit his Jesus in the Blessed Sacrament.

Francisco suffered a lot when he was ill.
He could not leave his house,
and spent his days lying down, very weak,
because he was very seriously ill.
Shortly before he died, the Parish Priest
brought him Holy Communion.
When he received Our Lord,
he spoke of his great joy
at having the 'hidden Jesus' in his breast.
The day Our Lady took him to Heaven,
he was smiling, and no longer suffering:
it was 4 April, 1919.
He was only ten years old.

Jacinta, too, became seriously ill
and Lucia used to visit her.
When she returned from Church
after going to Communion,
Jacinta used to hug her tightly,
because she knew that her cousin
had the hidden Jesus in her heart.
As she was not getting any better,
she was sent to the hospital
in Vila Nova de Ourem;
she then returned home until, later on,
she was transferred to a hospital in Lisbon.
Our Lady had told her
that she would have much to suffer,
that she would never again see her parents
or Lucia, and that she would die alone.

After many months of suffering,
Jacinta was indeed alone in a ward,
in the Hospital of D. Estefânia in Lisbon,
when Our Lady came to take her to Heaven
on 20th February 1920.

In the transept of the Basilica at the Shrine
of Our Lady of Fatima, the stones on
the tombs enclosing the mortal remains
of the two little shepherds
bear the simple legend:
"Franciso Marto to whom
Our Lady appeared".
"Jacinta Marto, to whom
Our Lady appeared."

The reputation for holiness
that the two children had acquired
during the last months of their lives
spread rapidly throughout the world
after their death.

FRANCISCO MARTO

a quem Nossa Senhora apareceu

JACINTA MARTO

a quem Nossa Senhora apareceu

On 13 May 1989, Pope John Paul II
solemnly recognised the heroic nature
of the virtues practised by Francisco and
Jacinta, and declared that they were models
of holiness, and powerful intercessors
for all the faithful, and especially for children.
On 28 June 1999, official recognition
of the miracle obtained
through their intercession
opened the way for their beatification.